The Christmas Craft Book

The Christmas Craft Book

Thomas Berger

Floris Books

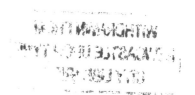

Translated by Polly Lawson

Photographs by Frits Dijkhof
Illustrations by Ronald Heuninck

First published in Dutch under the title *Kerstversieringen*
by Christofoor Publishers in 1990
First published in English in 1990 by Floris Books
This edition published in 2011

© 1990 Christofoor, Zeist
This translation © 1990 Floris Books

British Library CIP Data available
ISBN 978-086315-827-8
Printed in China

Contents

Foreword	7	Straw stars	41
Transparencies	9	Paper window stars	46
Candles	19	Pentagonal window stars	58
Advent calendars	22	Nativity scenes	61
Festive wreaths	25	Geometric decorations	66
Lanterns	28	Further reading	75
Angels	33	Resources	77

Foreword

Of all the festivals which we celebrate over the course of the year, Christmas has a special place. Once, many years ago, at the darkest and coldest time of the year, a shining host of angels appeared to shepherds in the fields to herald the birth of the long awaited Saviour. Through this event the whole of life upon earth has been profoundly changed.

This is the festival of the light that came to earth, the festival of the birth of the child Jesus. This is the festival which we celebrate afresh each year, which requires so much preparation, especially with children in the family.

The inner preparation for Christmas is best begun at the end of November or the beginning of December, which is the beginning of Advent, the month of expectation and preparation that leads up to Christmas. Some people start to celebrate Christmas during Advent by buying a Christmas tree early in December and decorating it immediately. It seems a shame to start celebrating Christmas so early in this way, since children are therefore deprived of Advent, which ought to lead them gradually to the great festival of light.

This book contains many Christmas decorations which you can make with children. By occupying ourselves and children in making these things, we create an atmosphere of preparation and expectation which fosters the spirit of Christmas in the soul of the child. In addition to various Advent calendars and motifs from the Gospel story, other Christmas elements are included: lanterns with their glowing light, transparencies through which the light can shine, folded transparent stars with their pattern of rays, and straw stars which irradiate a warm light through their smooth, golden-coloured surface. Several three-dimensional figures are also included, for the world of form and number also belongs to Christmas.

Few of the Christmas decorations contained in this book are original; they have been made in countless variations for many years. By collecting them together, and by showing how a decoration can be developed by making a very small modification, we hope to encourage you to try things out and develop your own variations.

A word of thanks is due here to the many people who have contributed to this book. Only a few have been named in the list of contents, but many parents of the children of the Vrije School in Zeist have helped with the making of Christmas decorations for this book.

Transparencies

MATERIALS
Coloured card (170 gsm)
Tissue paper
Tracing paper
Glue
Sharp scissors

The basic forms are transparencies *with a cardboard frame:* these are suitable for hanging in the window, or for standing on a table. And transparencies *without a frame:* the picture is made with coloured tissue paper stuck on to tracing paper, and is suitable for hanging in a window.

When making transparencies it is best to start with a white background. A glass table with a lamp under it or a box with a light inside it are useful when making transparencies.

When choosing the colours remember that mixed colours will appear when two layers of different coloured tissue paper are laid over one another. Sometimes the result is quite surprising!

Draw the outlines on tissue paper with a sharp pencil. When you are cutting out the forms the pencil lines must be cut away too.

When cutting out the forms use a small pair of sharp scissors and take plenty of time because it is not as easy as it looks.

When gluing layers together use as little glue as possible and spread it as thinly as possible; blobs remain visible. Water-based glue is quite adequate and can be undone if necessary. However, one disadvantage is that the sheets become unstuck after a time. You can also use a glue stick.

Transparencies which are hung on the window can get damaged by condensation. Put a plastic sheet between the window and the transparency to avoid damage.

SIMPLE TRANSPARENCY WITH A FRAME

These simple transparencies can be hung in front of the window. Any subject can be depicted. The simplest transparency is shown in Figure 1 where the picture of Easter rabbits is cut out of card and a single coloured piece of tissue paper is stuck to the back.

Draw the shape of the frame as well as the inside design on the back of a piece of strong, coloured card.

Cut out the outside frame of the transparency.

Cut out the picture inside with a pair of sharp scissors or a sharp knife.

Stick a sheet of tissue paper on to the back of the card frame (the side on which there are pencil marks).

Make a loop to hang the transparency with a needle and thread.

1 Simple transparency with frame

9

'STAINED GLASS' TRANSPARENCY

This technique gives the effect of stained glass panes set in lead (Figures 2 and 3).

1. First draw the design and the frame of the transparency on white tracing paper and then transfer the forms to the (dark blue) drawing paper by using carbon paper; or you can draw the design straight on to the drawing paper (Figure 5).

2. Cut out the design and the framework using sharp scissors or a knife.

3. Lay tissue paper of the chosen colours on top of the drawing on the white tracing paper. The outlines of the drawing will be visible through the tissue paper. With a pencil trace the figures or details appropriate to this colour on to the tissue paper. Make the outlines on the tissue paper a little bigger than the original outlines on the drawing.

4. Cut out the figures on the coloured tissue paper and stick them on to the back of the blue drawing paper using as little glue as possible. You can use a matchstick to smear a tiny bit of glue along the edges of the drawing.

In this way stick colour by colour to the frame. When two colours of tissue paper overlap new colours are created.

Finally stick the transparency on to the window with two tiny strips of double-sided adhesive tape.

2 'Stained glass' transparency

3 'Stained glass' transparency

4 'Stained glass' triptych

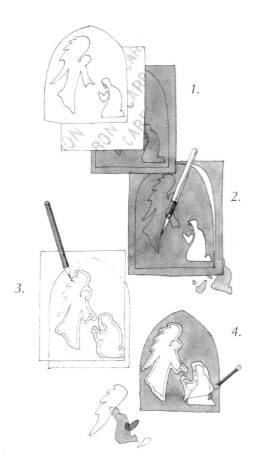

5 Making a stained-glass transparency

6 and 7 Window triptych

'STAINED GLASS' TRIPTYCH

Make a simple triptych (Figure 4) in the same way as the previous transparency. You can put this on a table or shelf with a night-light behind it.

Once you have cut out the frame, crease it with a blunt knife or dried-up ballpoint pen to make neat folds.

WINDOW TRIPTYCH

Instead of the stained glass window effect you can cut out a big window in the frame and fill it with several colours of tissue paper. This can be done in two ways:

1. In Figure 6 the boy is cut out of the card frame as a silhouette, and coloured tissue paper is added behind.

2. In Figure 7 Mary, Joseph and the donkey are cut out of card and then covered with tissue paper. The background is added behind.

Cut the outside shape from card and crease the folds with a blunt knife or dried-out ballpoint pen. Cut out the inside shape.

Trace the opening onto a sheet of tracing paper. Then tear the shapes you want in the background from coloured tissue paper. Stick the pieces of tissue paper on to the tracing paper and slowly build up the transparency layer by layer.

Finally cut out the tracing paper (with the design) about 1 cm ($1/2$ in) wider than the edge of the frame, and stick it to the back of the card frame with the tissue paper to the front.

FRAMELESS TRANSPARENCY

Draw the shape of the transparency on to a sheet of tracing paper. Lay it on a light table, or stick it to the window.

Figure 8 has been made by tearing the tissue paper. If you are not confident of making a freehand picture, draw the picture on paper and lay it under the tracing paper. Tearing the paper instead of cutting gives a very free effect. Only rarely will you need to tear a piece into an exact shape (like the sword). Using different layers and colours of tissue paper will give rich colour shadings and depth.

LAYERED TRANSPARENCIES

The technique described here uses only tissue paper, which allows the colours full scope and provides endless variations.

The angel in Figure 9 is made from two layers of yellow tissue paper and a layer of white tissue paper as a cover.

First draw the design onto white tracing paper.

1. Then for each layer of tissue paper draw the required part of the design onto a separate sheet of tracing paper. The yellow angel consists of the different elements shown in Figure 11. Lay the first sheet of yellow tissue paper on top of the first drawing and with a sharp pencil trace the figure. Cut it out.

2. Lay the cut-out sheet on the second drawing and move it around until the two drawings fit. Then lay the second sheet of yellow tissue paper exactly over the first, put the second drawing over and cut it out.Stick the two sheets together only at the edges at a few points, and do the same with the white sheet of tissue paper. Finally, stick down any loose ends with a tiny bit of glue.

8 Frameless transparency

9 Layered transparency

10 Layered transparency variation

The blue angel in Figure 10 has one layer more than the yellow angel (Figure 11, step 3): this transparency consists of two layers of light blue and one layer of pink or mauve tissue paper. The method is the same.

When sticking them together make sure that the cut-out figures fit exactly over each other; the outside edge can be trimmed later.

1.

2.

3.

11 Making a layered transparency

13

TRANSPARENCIES WITH PARTITIONS

MATERIALS
Gold card
Thick and thin white card
Tissue paper in various colours
Tracing paper
Scissors or a knife
Glue
2 sheets of blue paper (A4 or letter, not too thin)

A transparency built with several partitions, with spaces between, gives a wonderful perspective and a deeper dimension. You can place a candle or light behind or in front for a good effect.

12. Partition transparency

13. Simple partition transparency

14. Transparency with roof

Figures 12, 13 and 14 show three different transparencies with partitions. The first two are made in the same way.

The transparency in Figure 12 consists of a gold frame in front of the first partition, a narrow mid-partition which simply indicates the ground, and the back partition. The transparency in Figure 13 is more complex with three mid-partitions. The stable in Figure 14 relies on the same principle, but it has a roof and the partitions are fixed in a different way.

the number of partitions is partly determined by the intended design. The fact that on the left hand side of the transparency in Figure 13, two shepherds and Mary have been placed one behind the other means that three mid-partitions are necessary. Bear this in mind when you are designing your transparency. It is technically possible to make more partitions, but it does not necessarily make the transparency more beautiful.

By following the instructions below for making the transparency in Figure 13, you will understand the principle and be able to make other versions.

Begin by sketching the whole picture with all the objects and figures. Do this at the size the transparency will be. A good size is 20 cm (18 in) high by 25 cm (10 in) wide.

Decide how many partitions will be necessary for your sketch. To make the operation easier give each partition a number, beginning at the front. The transparency of Figure 13 has five partitions (Figure 15). If you are inexperienced in making these transparencies, it is best to draw each partition with all the figures belonging to it first to make sure they fit.

Determine the outer shape of the transparency and so of all the partition frames. Cut the frame for the first partition from gold card. Make this one slightly larger than the others, which will recede into the background behind it. Cut the other frames from thick white card, each slightly smaller than the one in front, following the diagrams in Figure 15. Cut out the inside of each partition, making sure the ground becomes progressively higher as you go back; this increases the perspective. These frames do not have any trees or figures but should include the stable's timber frame.

Cut out the people and animals from the thinner white card, and in this case also the crib. Make the figures narrower than you want them to be because they will be dressed with tissue paper. Fold the tissue-paper clothes and stick them on loosely, making sure that the clothes project beyond the figures. Sticking the clothes on loosely so that they billow (see Mary and Joseph in Figure 12) will bring the picture to life.

When dressing, begin with the face and hands, then stick on the clothing. The foremost shepherd's crook is stuck to his hand after he has been dressed. Also the child is cut out separately before being placed in the crib (Figure 16, p.17).

With the ox and ass draw only the visible parts (Figure 16b), cover them in flat tissue paper then stick them straight into the stable. The lamb in the foreground is covered with little wads of white tissue paper.

The people and animals are now dressed, but the partitions are still bare.

Partition 2 (Figure 15) has moss and grass. When you are sticking it together remember that the tissue paper must protrude beyond the cardboard frame at the top.

This applies also to partition 3, where you can add a tree with green tissue paper at the side.

Partition 4 is more difficult. Begin by sticking blue tissue paper around the outside of the stable to make the sky. Only when the glue is dry cut out the star and its rays from the blue tissue paper using a sharp knife. Stick yellow tissue paper behind to form the starry sky. Cover the timbers of the stable with dark yellow tissue paper.

Cover partition 5 wholly with white tracing paper. Now cover the stable section with light yellow tissue paper. You can darken it and add texture in places by overlapping several layers of tissue paper at the back of the partition, so that the transparency becomes progressively darker towards the edges (Figure 16c). Leave the space above the stable nice and light so that the candlelight can shine on to the star in partition 4. Now stick the figures into their places. The crib is placed in the middle of partition 4, with Mary and Joseph on each side, while the animals look on from the sides between the timbers; two shepherds are placed a little wider on partition 3, and the standing shepherd and lamb are stuck to partition 2.

Cut two pieces from blue paper and fold them together like a concertina (Figure 16d). Stick the partitions together at both sides using the folded strips, making sure that there is always at least one zigzag between the folded strips.

In the transparency described here, we have allowed more space between the second and third partition because this shepherd is still in the field and not in the stable. The depth of the transparency should now be 8–10 cm (3–4 in). This prevents it from falling over. In the simple

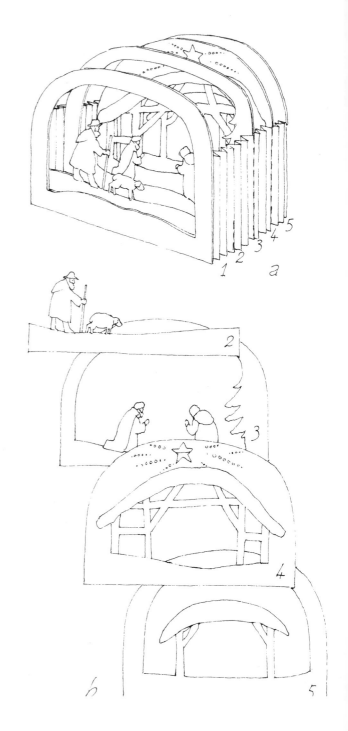

15. *Design for a partition transparency*

16

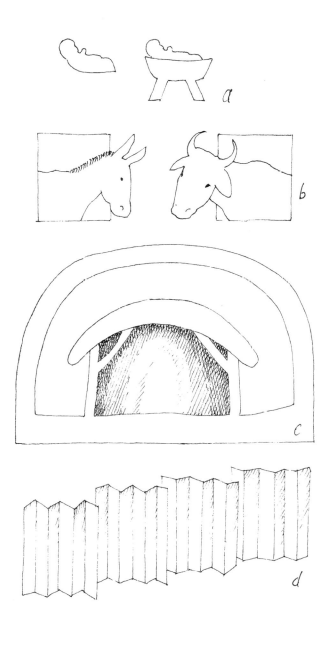

partition transparency of Figure 12, the gap between the three partitions is made bigger to give the transparency stability.

Figure 14 shows a stable with a roof. This transparency is made in the same way as described above, but the partitions are joined together with flat pieces of cardboard stuck to the side (Figure 17). First stick all the partitions together before attaching the roof and doors of the stable. Then stick the stable to the backing section when everything is finished. In this case, you can also add individual figures in front of the stable.

Whereas the partitions of the other two transparencies create an effect of spaciousness, here the enclosed space of the stable is made by making the inside of the first partition smaller, done here with timbers.

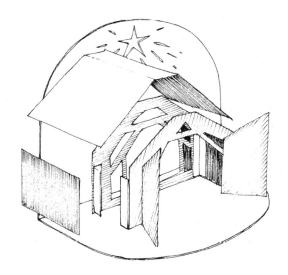

16. Additional sections

17. Making a transparency with a roof

Candles

DIPPING CANDLES

Candles are used mainly in wintertime when it's dark, though they can be used for special occasions throughout the year. When decorating them you can choose a motif for the festival of the season.

MATERIALS
Beeswax or candle stubs
Candle wick or a thick cotton yarn
Tall narrow tins
Pan of hot water
Hotplate or spirit stove

Dipping candles requires a lot of patience. Hot water and molten wax are very hot! Young children should only dip candles under adult supervision.

Put some water in a saucepan to boil. Put the bits of wax or candle stubs in a tall narrow tin, and place the tin into the pan of heating water to melt the wax. The depth of the wax in the tin will determine the maximum length of the candles. When the wax has melted, the pan can be transferred to a hotplate or spirit stove on the table.

Lay some newspaper underneath to catch any spilt candle grease. Keep topping up the water to replace what has evaporated.

Wax takes a long time to melt and as it then slowly solidifies on the hotplate it is a good idea to have a second tin of melted wax ready to hand.

For the wick, cut a length of candle wick or cotton yarn long enough to prevent children getting their fingers in the hot wax. Before dipping pull the wick taut with both hands so that the finished candle will be straight.

Dip the wick into the hot wax for a moment, draw it out again and allow the wax on it to set before dipping the wick in again. In this way a new layer is added each time.

At the base of the candle a blob of wax will form and grow bigger each time the candle is dipped. Cut this blob off with a knife from time to time.

Once the candle is finished leave it to cool and harden. This can take several hours, so it is a good idea to hang the candle up by the wick to prevent it being damaged (Figure 18).

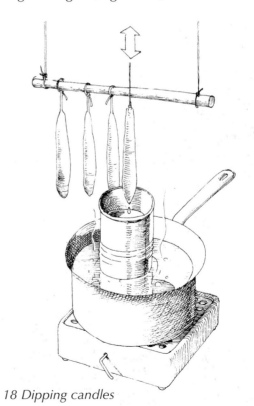

18 Dipping candles

Opposite: 19–24 Decorated candles

DECORATING CANDLES

Thick candle
Candle decorating wax in various colours
Thick knitting needle or spatula

As you can see from Figures 19–24, candles can be decorated using various techniques. In each case the decorating wax must first be made workable.

Take small pieces and knead them well until the wax is warm and soft.

The simplest method of decorating candles is to stick little bits of coloured wax on to the candle and then work them into shape.

You can use a spatula or knitting needle to shape the finer details. New colours can be made by thoroughly kneading two different coloured bits of wax together (as for example red and yellow making orange).

Make sure that the coloured wax is properly warmed when you press it on to the candle otherwise it will not stick on properly and may come unstuck later.

DECORATING CANDLES BY SMEARING

MATERIALS
Thick candle (off-white or white)
Fine sandpaper
Candle decorating wax in various colours
Thick knitting needle or spatula

Use a piece of fine sandpaper to roughen the place on the candle where you wish to add the decoration.

Warm a small piece of wax between your fingers beginning with the lightest colour. Press a little wax on to the candle and smear it out very thinly with your warm fingers to give a transparent effect. Now layer the darker colours carefully over the lighter ones.

Use a knitting needle or a spatula to define the details; by scratching the wax or by pulling it up you can make forms in relief. Kneading different colours together for a long time will produce new colours.

The colours black, white, gold and silver are not transparent and so are used less in this method.

This technique requires some practice, but does give a very special effect.

CLAY CANDLESTICKS

MATERIALS
Clay
Candle
Watercolours and paintbrush
Transparent varnish
Sprigs of greenery

During Advent, modelling can be a wonderful occupation, and you can make candlesticks with a great variety of shapes: for instance, a simple cube, or an angel carrying a candle between the wings (Figure 25). Put a little saucer underneath to catch the candle wax and avoid it dripping on to the table or your clothes.

Make the candlestick out of one piece of clay. Any bits that you stick on may come unstuck when the candlestick dries.

Although you can make the candle hole to fit a particular candle, you must take the candle out of the hole while the clay is still wet because it contracts while drying and can split if the candle is left in.

Decorate the candlestick: you can stick sprigs of fir, holly, gold-painted acorns, etc. in the clay while it is still soft, and in this way it becomes a Christmas table decoration. Make sure that the sprigs are not too close to the candle flame.

Allow the candlestick to dry out thoroughly and then you can paint it with watercolours. Once the paint is dry the candlestick can be varnished.

Figure 26 shows a Michaelmas candlestick in the shape of a dragon.

25 Cube and angel candlesticks

26 Dragon candlestick

21

Advent calendars

Advent begins on the fourth Sunday before Christmas and lasts till Christmas itself. If Christmas Eve is on a Saturday, the first Sunday in Advent will fall on November 27, and Advent lasts for four full weeks. If Christmas Eve is on a Sunday, the first Sunday in Advent will fall on December 3, and the fourth Sunday of Advent coincides with Christmas Eve. Before you make an Advent calendar count the number of days in Advent in that year.

There are many kinds of Advent calendars. The most common are those in which a child opens one door for each day of Advent. Advent calendars help children anticipate Christmas, enabling them to count the days, and in some versions making the approach of Christmas visible. Advent is the festival of expectation. The colour blue can be seen to express expectation, so it is an appropriate colour for Advent.

ADVENT LADDER

MATERIALS

Blue card about 25 × 35 cm (10 × 14 in)
2 wooden slats approximately 310 mm long x 7 mm wide (12^1/4 × ^{1}/4 in)
Gold card
Gold paper
Pink beeswax
Half a walnut shell
Unspun sheep's wool
Glue

Round off the top corners of the blue card (Figure 27).

Sandpaper the slats till they are smooth and stick them to the middle of the blue card about 1 cm (^{3}/8 in) from the bottom and 6 cm (2^3/8 in) apart.

Cut two long struts 1 cm (^{3}/8 in) wide and 31 cm (12^1/4 in) long, and as many golden rungs 7 × 0.4 cm (2^3/4 × ^{3}/16 in) from the gold card as there are days in Advent, including the first Sunday of Advent and Christmas Eve.

Before sticking on the rungs, mark their places on the wooden slats — the distance between each rung should be about 13 mm (^{1}/2 in). Stick the rungs on, starting at the top and working down. Once all the rungs are firmly glued on, stick the gold card struts on to the slats so that they cover the rung-ends. Round off the tops of the struts which project beyond the slats.

Model the figure of a baby from beeswax so that it can lodge between the rungs. It is advisable to make the child from one piece rather than making limbs separately and then attaching them.

Place the walnut shell with a little sheep's wool in it at the bottom of the ladder for the crib.

From the gold paper cut out as many stars as there are days in Advent. Each day the children can stick a star on the blue sky behind the ladder as the child descends a rung. On Christmas Day the child lies in the crib, with a sky full of stars behind him.

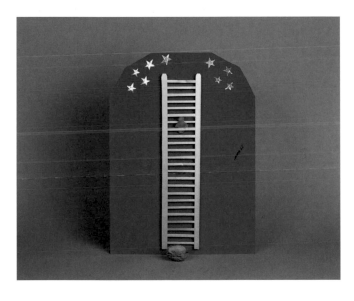

27 Advent ladder

STAR RIBBON

MATERIALS
130 cm (4 ft) dark blue ribbon 2 cm (3/4 in) wide
Silver card
Gold card
Straw
Fine gold thread
Glue

For this calendar, ribbon and stars make a kind of stairway down which an angel can come. Each Sunday in Advent is marked by a straw star and the six days between are marked by silver stars; the ladder begins with the first straw star.

As with the Advent ladder, count the number of days in Advent for the year. Stars should be made for the right number of days.

The construction of straw stars is fully described from page 41 and there is a pattern for a five-pointed star on page 30.

First lay out the straw stars and the silver card stars beside the ribbon to ensure that the distance between the stars is roughly the same.

Stick all the stars to the ribbon, making sure that you only glue the middle of the star and the points are not stuck down.

Finally, cut out an angel from the gold card. Beginning on the first Sunday of Advent, the angel comes down one step each day, and can be tucked in neatly behind the stars.

You can place a crib at the bottom of the ribbon, or you can hang the ribbon above a stable scene where at Christmas the child will be born.

Advent Walnut Chain

MATERIALS

As many walnuts as there are days in Advent
Gold paint
3–4 metres (yards) of red or blue ribbon 2 cm (3/4 in) wide
Small presents to put in the nutshells
Glue

Open the nuts carefully so you don't crack or break the shells. Remove the kernel. Keep the two halves of each nut together so that they don't get muddled up.

Paint the outside of the nutshells gold and leave them to dry. In one half of each nut place a small present such as a little bell, a dwarf, a shell, a little sheep, a little stone, a little lump of beeswax, a marble, a gold-foil star, a dried flower, a bead and so on.

Apply a little glue to each half and stick them together with the ribbon running through the two halves.

During Advent a nut is cut off the ribbon each day and opened.

Starry Sky Advent Calendar

MATERIALS

Big sheet of dark blue sugar paper or card
Gold paper for stars
Glue
Scissors

Round off corners of the blue card to indicate the vault of heaven. Place the card in a suitable place: pin it to the wall, or it can form the background of a tableau for a Christmas crib.

On each day of Advent children are allowed to stick a star in the sky, forming a glorious starry sky background to the Christmas crib.

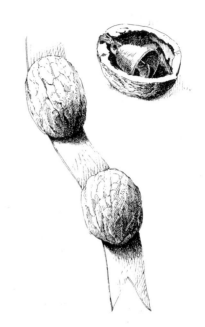

28 Advent walnut chain

29 Advent wreath

Festive wreaths

Advent wreath

Materials
Thick wire (2 mm, $1/16$ in) for the hoop
Thin wire (1 mm, $1/32$ in) for the candle holders
Sprigs of green fir
Waxed thread or string
4 candles
Blue ribbon

1. Take a piece of thick wire, more than twice the circumference of the Advent wreath, to make a double hoop (Figure 30). Twist the ends firmly together.

2. Cover the frame with greenery. Start by making a foundation with larger twigs, 20–25 cm (8–10 in). Lay the bottom of the first stem against the hoop and bind it on with the waxed thread or fine string. Lay the next twig underneath the first so that it is overlapped by the first and bind it on. Continue in this way so that the wreath gradually increases in thickness.

3. After the first round use smaller sprigs which are less stiff and more easily bound on. For the last round use short pretty sprigs to give a smooth and even effect.

4. For each of the four candle holders take a piece of thin wire and wind it several times round the bottom of a candle and then bend the two ends down.

Place the candle holders on four points of the wreath, making sure that they don't disappear into the greenery but remain visible. Bend the protruding ends of wire round the bottom of the wreath (Figure 29).

Cut the blue ribbon in two equal lengths. Tie the ends of both ribbons on to the wreath midway between the candles. Suspend the Advent wreath by the ribbon. Alternatively you can wind the blue ribbon around the wreath as a decoration.

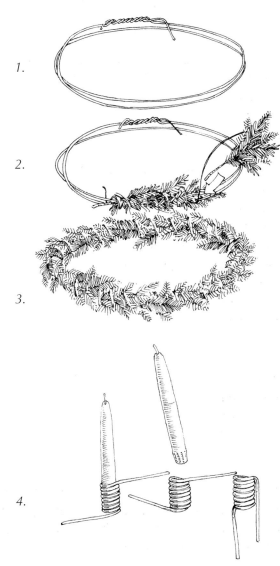

30 Making an advent or door wreath

PINE CONE WREATH

MATERIALS
7 pine cones of the same size
Thin wire
Ribbon
Pliers

1. Lay the seven well-dried pine cones out in a circle and measure a length of wire 2½ times the circumference of the circle of cones (Figure 32).

2. Bend the wire double.

3. Make an eye at the bend by twisting the wire round several times. The eye is to suspend the wreath. The length of twisted wire between the eye and the first cone should be about 1 cm (½ in).

4. Push the wire between the scales of the first cone about a quarter of the way up from the bottom, twist the wire a few times so that the pine cone sits firmly between the wires.

5. Attach the other cones in the same way.

Make sure you twist the wire sufficiently between each cone so that they are not too close together, otherwise you will not be able to bend the wire round to make a wreath.

Once all seven cones have been attached, bend the whole thing round to make a wreath. Twist the end of the wire a few times round the eye and cut off.

Finish off the wreath by tying a bow with ribbon under the eye (Figure 31). You could also tie in some greenery.

31 Pine cone wreath

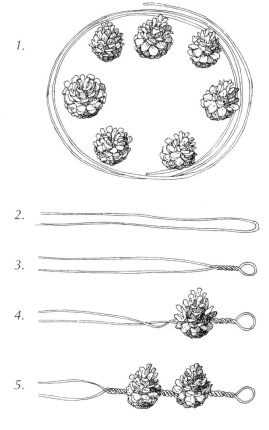

32 Making a pine-cone wreath

Door wreath

MATERIALS
Waxed thread or string
Fir sprigs
Coniferous greenery
Wire 1.5 mm (³/64 in)
Decoration, such as holly leaves, ivy, berries,
    pine and larch cones, lichen

Make a ring of wire about 25 cm (10 in) in diameter, twisting the ends firmly together (Figure 33). First attach some larger fir sprigs (20–25 cm, 8–10 in long) as described for the Advent wreath (Figure 30).

Use plenty of greenery and pull the wire tight. Avoid protruding twigs. After the foundation of fir twigs continue with coniferous greenery until the wreath has been built up evenly all round. Continue building the wreath using the wire for support and covering any visible parts of the wire. Use smaller sprigs of greenery and arrange them evenly with an overlap. Pay attention to the blend of colours.

Attach pine cones, larch cones, berries and lichen, by winding a 15 cm (6 in) piece of wire under the lowest row of scales on the cone. Pull the wire tight and twist it round a few times with a pair of pliers before binding it to the wreath. Lichen can be attached similarly.

Finally tie a coloured ribbon to the wreath by which it can be suspended.

33 Door wreath

Lanterns

A SIMPLE LANTERN

MATERIALS
Thin drawing paper (120 gsm)
Watercolours and brush
Salad oil
Glue
Wide jam jar
Candle

The lantern consists of a loose cuff of paper placed over the jam jar (Figure 34, step 1).

Wet the paper, lay it on a board and smooth it out by wiping a wet sponge over it.

Paint the wet paper with watercolours. Don't paint a picture, just create a mood with the colours.

Allow the paper to dry and oil both sides of the paper sparingly with cooking oil.

Cut the paper to the right size. The depth of the paper should be slightly more (but not more than 1 cm, 1/2 in) than the height of the glass. The length of the paper should be about 2 cm (3/4 in) more than the circumference of the glass.

Glue the ends of the paper together to make a cylinder which will fit easily over the glass jar.

Place a night-light or a small candle in the jar and the lantern is finished.

VARIATION
Instead of the jar use a round Camembert cheese box. Cut away half of the (usually high) rim and remove the top of the lid (Figure 34, step 2).

Glue the upper and lower rims and stick the painted paper first to the bottom half and then to the top half of the cheese box. Finally glue the vertical edges of the paper together.

Take a strip of aluminium foil, fold it several times, and wrap it round a small candle, so that it extends below the candle. Make several cuts in the foil so that it can be spread open in rays and glue them to the bottom of the lantern.

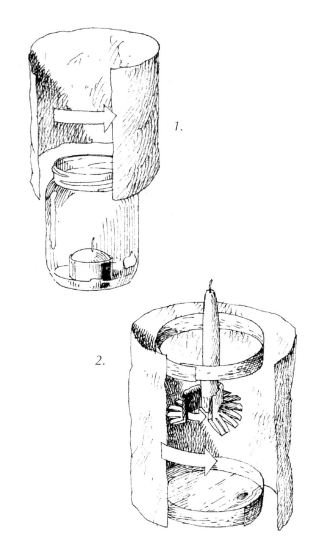

34 Making simple lanterns

Glass jar lantern

MATERIALS
Large glass jar (2 litre, 2 quarts)
Tissue paper in various colours
Gold card
An old cloth
Wallpaper paste
Sharp knife or needle

Glue a layer of white tissue paper around the outside of the jar as a base for the transparency. It does not need to be smooth all over.

Copy the picture in Figure 35 or sketch your own design on a piece of paper. Don't make the figures too small.

Tear or cut the garments out of tissue paper. Stick the figures flat on the white tissue paper. Put a fold or two in the clothes. Kings can have golden crowns on their heads and even golden staffs in their hands.

Use blue tissue paper for the sky. To make a starry sky scratch out stars here and there with a sharp knife or big needle.

A large jar needs a bigger candle. A night-light is too dim.

35 Glass jar lantern

Star lantern

MATERIALS
Strong drawing paper (170 gsm)
Pair of compasses or protractor
Ruler
Craft knife
Night-light
Glue stick

This lantern is made up of eleven pentagons. Use the pattern in Figure 37 to cut out the size you require.

You can paint the paper with watercolours before drawing the pentagons and cutting them out.

Continued overleaf

36 Star lantern

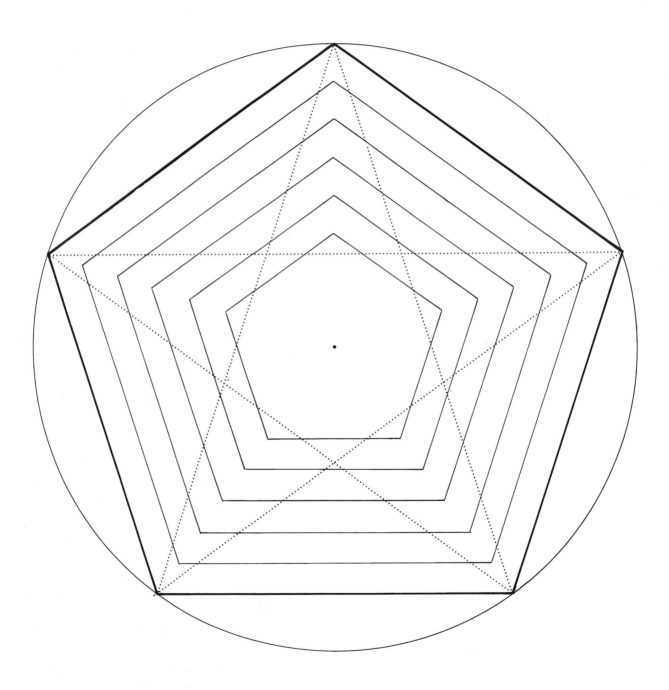

30

1. Bisect all the sides of the pentagons. Join these points together, scoring along the lines lightly with a knife (Figure 38).

2. Fold in the triangles you have made to make a smaller pentagon.

3. Stick the pentagons together in such a way that the flaps — the folded corners — always overlap the adjoining pentagon.

4. First construct the bottom half from the base and then build up the upper edge by sticking the pentagons point downward on to the bottom half. For the opening at the top, stick the flaps down inside. Do the same at the bottom if you don't wish to have a base; without a base the candle or night-light is more easily lit.

When the candle is lit inside the lantern, a five-pointed star becomes visible in every pentagon (Figure 36).

Opposite: 37 Pentagons

Right: 38 Making a star lantern

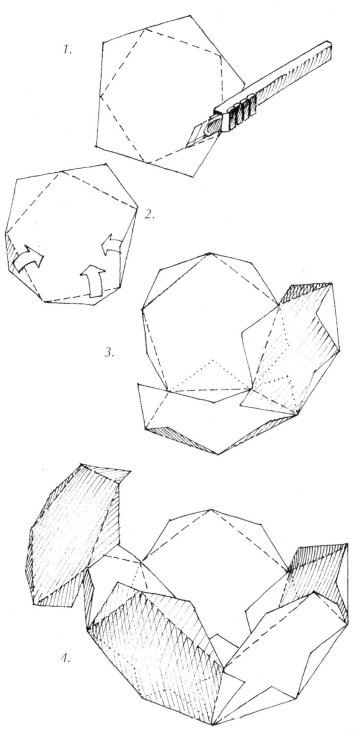

31

DODECAHEDRON LANTERN

MATERIALS

Strong drawing paper (160 gsm)
Pair of compasses or protractor
Ruler
Craft knife
Glue stick

This lantern looks like the star lantern, but without the 5-pointed stars.

Make smaller pentagons with sides of 5 cm (2 in). The pattern in Figure 37 gives you an exact pentagon. Figure 115 (page 67) shows (at 60% of true size) how to cut several pentagons from one sheet, to save sticking them together (ignore the odd sixth one in Figure 115).

1. Cut out two lots of five pentagons, adding extra flaps at *a* (Figure 39). Fold the flaps inwards and glue them to each other. In this way they are invisible when the light shines through.

2. Stick the pentagons of the top and bottom halves together by folding their flaps inward in the same way.

This lantern can be painted before drawing and cutting out the pentagons or it can be covered with tissue paper (Figure 40).

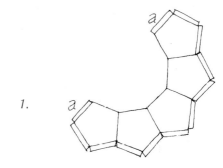

1.

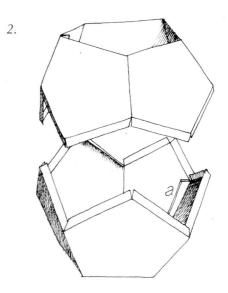

2.

Right: 39 Making a dodecahedron

Above: 40 Dodecahedron lantern

Angels

WOOLLEN ANGEL

MATERIALS

Unspun sheep's wool, about 45 cm (18 in) in
length
Thin gold or silver thread

1. When working with upspun sheep's wool, don't
cut it but gently tease it apart (Figure 42).

2. Separate off one third of the wool for the
arms and wings of the angel.

3. Tie a knot in the middle of the thicker skein
and pull it tight. This becomes the face.

4. Hold the skein vertically, letting the wool
above the knot fall down.

5. Spread this wool round the head as hair and
secure at the neck with a long gold thread. Tie the
ends of the gold thread together to make a loop
for suspending the figure.

6. Lay the angel face down. Take the wool
which you have just brought down for hair and
divide it into three parts. Bring the middle part
back up over the head; bring the other two parts
to the sides — they will shortly become the wings.

7. For one of the arms separate off a bit of
wool about 15 cm (6 in) long from the thin skein.
Twist the wool firmly together in the middle, fold
the skein double and tie up the hand with gold
thread. Do not cut off the fluff forming the arms.
Make the other arm in the same way.

8. Keeping the angel face down, place the arms
under the neck and bring the tuft of wool which
you laid over the head down over the arms.

41 Woollen angel

9. Turn the angel over, push the arms and wings
well up, and tie up the body firmly under the
arms with a length of gold thread. Allow the ends
to hang down as tassels from the belt.

Fluff the wings and robe into shape by holding
the wool firmly in one hand and teasing it out
carefully with the other (Figure 41).

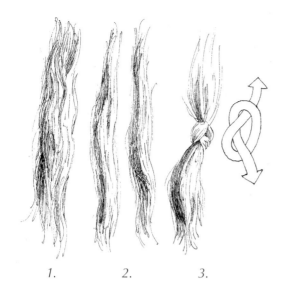

1.   2.   3.

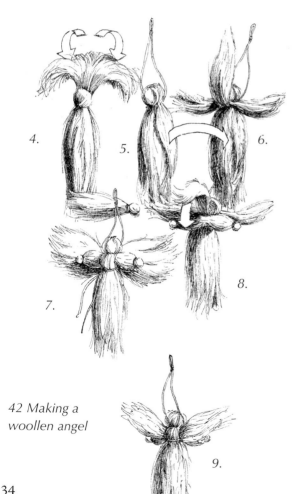

4.   5.   6.

7.   8.

42 Making a woollen angel

9.

ANGEL MOBILE

MATERIALS
White tissue paper
Unspun sheep's wool
Gold thread
White yarn
Fine silver wire
Walnut shell
White beeswax
Glue
Scissors
Pliers

Cut out two squares 18 × 18 cm (7 × 7 in) from tissue paper. Lay one of the squares shiny side down on the table with one of the corners pointing away from you (Figure 43).

1. Fold the left and right corners 2.5 cm (1 in) inwards.

2. Put a blob of wool the size of a big marble in the middle of the square.

3. Fold the paper over the blob so that the two opposite corners meet.

4. Shape the blob and tie off the head with white thread.

5. Make hands out of the two corners of the paper and tie them up with white thread. Give the angel shape, making the upper part billow out so that she really appears to sweep through the air.

Take two lengths of gold thread 20 cm (8 in) and tie each end to a hand (Figure 44). Tie the other ends of the threads together and glue them to the rim of the walnut shell. Take care that the threads are of equal length.

Make a second angel in the same way and glue the threads to the other side of the walnut.

Cut a length of 17 cm (7 in) from the silver wire and bend back both ends of the wire with pliers to make loops. Bend the wire to make a slight bow. Tie a gold thread about 17 cm (7 in) long round the neck of both angels, and tie these threads to the wire loops. Tie a gold thread to the middle of the wire to suspend the mobile.

Stuff a tuft of wool into the walnut shell (which can be painted gold) and lay a little beeswax child in it. Now the angels can bear the child down from heaven to the earth.

You could make the angels independently, or alternatively make a mobile with more angels.

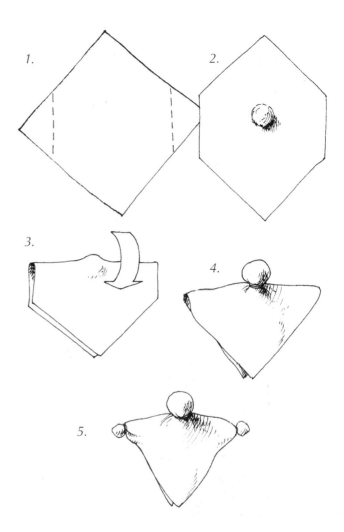

43 Making a paper angel

44 Angel mobile

35

STRAW ANGEL

MATERIALS
Straw
Strong thread or gold thread
Adhesive tape
Gold foil
Glue
Scissors

See page 141 for various ways of preparing straw.

For the *head* and *body* use un-ironed round straw.

For the *arms* use ironed straw.

For the *wings* use straw which has been cut open and ironed flat.

Take about eight un-ironed round stalks and allow them to soak in a basin of water for several hours to make them more pliant. Follow the steps in Figure 46.

1. Bend the straw over in the middle. The length of the halved straws now makes up the head, body and lower half of the angel.

2. Tie off the head with a strong thread.

3. Take three or four ironed (not cut open) straws and insert them between the round straws of the body to form the arms.

4. Tie off the body.

5. Now form the straws which make up the lower part of the angel into a round bell shape using something round, for example a medicine bottle or a candle (diameter 1.5–2 cm, 3/4 in). Insert it into the bottom of the bell of straws, so that the wet straws are made to stand out. Stick the straw on to the medicine bottle with adhesive tape that can be removed easily afterwards.

Allow the straw to dry overnight in this position and next day remove the tape. The straw will now form a round bell shape.

6. Trim the bottom with scissors, but don't cut too much off. Test whether the angel will stand properly by placing her on the table.

Finish off the arms by gluing the arm straws together and bending them forward before the glue dries.

At this point the angel should still have very long arms. In fact you can now tie these arms together with a bit of string to hold them in front. Once the glue is completely dry trim the arms to the proper length and make hands by tying the ends of the straw together with thread.

7. While the angel's body is drying you can make the wings. Take flat, opened stalks of the same colour. Lay them across each other in a fan shape and glue them together. Dry them under pressure, so that the fan is as flat as possible. You can use adhesive tape here to keep the wings in shape.

Before attaching the wings, dress the angel with a girdle made of a strip of gold foil (Figure 45), with two golden bands crossing over the breast, or with a golden headband which can have a star.

8. Glue the fan on to the back of the angel's body to form the wings. When the glue is dry clip the wings to the correct shape.

The number of straw stems determines the thickness of the angel. Don't use less than eight stalks for the body or the lower part will be too thin.

Opposite, near right: 45 Straw angel

Opposite, far right : 46 Making a straw angel

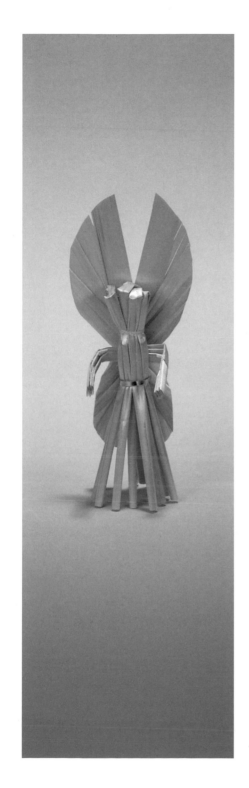

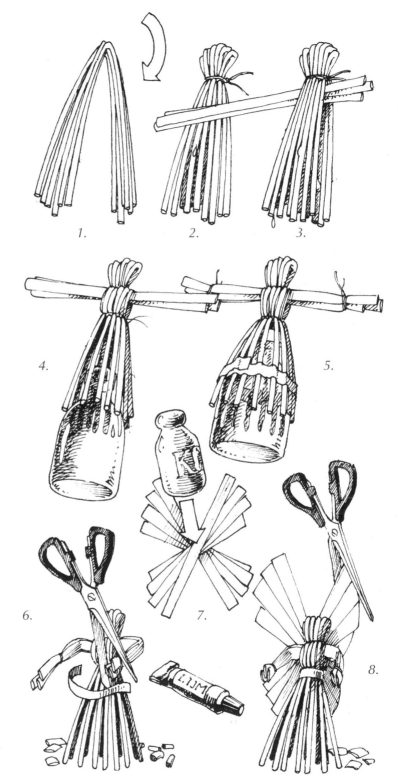

1.

2.

3.

4.

5.

6.

7.

8.

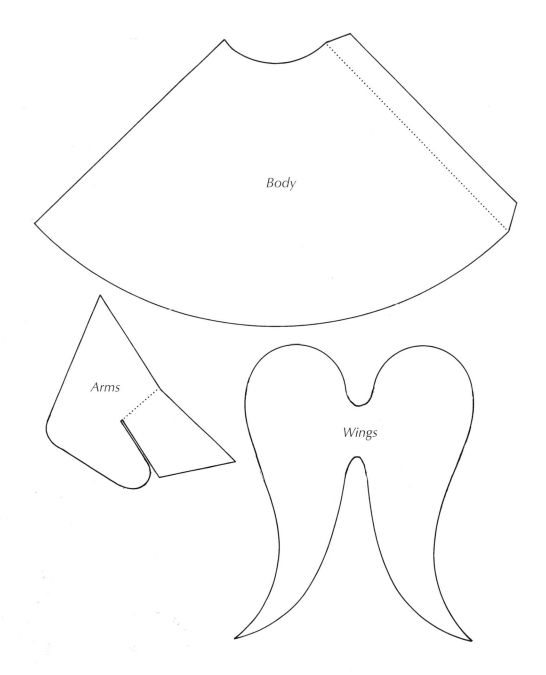

Body

Arms

Wings

47 Pattern for foil angel

FOIL ANGEL

MATERIALS
White tissue paper
Unspun sheep's wool
Gold foil
Blunt needle or fine knitting needle
Glue

Start by cutting out the pieces for the body, arms and wings from gold foil. Now follow the steps in Figure 49.

1. Cut a square piece of tissue paper 10 × 10 cm (4 × 4 in) for the head (Figure 47). Place a small ball of unspun sheep's wool in the centre.

2. Fold the paper over the ball to make a head.

3. Tie the head at the neck with thread.

4. To decorate the foil body and wings as shown in Figure 48, lay the foil with the shiny outside facing up on a base of soft cardboard. Draw shapes on using a blunt needle or a fine knitting needle.

5. Attach the head by placing the neck inside the body and sticking the two edges of the body together to make a funnel shape.

6. Stick the arms to both sides of the body, and the wings to the back. Take a little tuft of teased sheep's wool, spread this round the head for hair and glue it on. Finally make two little hands of tissue paper and stick these to the arms.

48 Foil angel

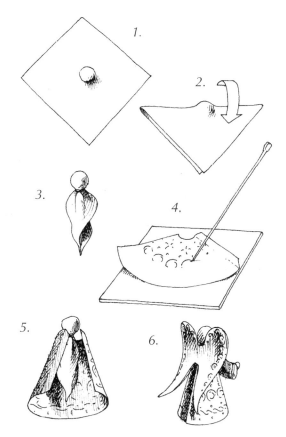

49 Making a foil angel

Straw stars

MATERIALS
Natural-coloured straw
Sharp knife
Pointed scissors
Basin of water
An iron

Soak the straw in water for about an hour. For flat straw, cut down into the tops a little way with a sharp knife and iron them open further with a hot iron. You can also leave the wet straws uncut and hollow, and just iron them flat.

You can use both flat and hollow stalks, and make them into very wide or very narrow strips (cut with a ruler and a sharp knife). Straw stars made of flat straws have the disadvantage that they have a good side and a bad side, so they look best against a background.

Straw stars made from hollow straw are the same on both sides, and are more suitable for mobiles, for use on the Christmas tree or to be hung in front of a window.

In the examples given in this book gold thread is always used for suspending the stars, but any other colour can be used, for instance, red.

Cut the stalks into two or three lengths depending on the size of the star.

8-POINTED STAR

1. Lay two stalks of equal length crosswise upon each other (Figure 59).

2. Add another two diagonal stalks. Put your forefinger on the point where the stalks cross each other to hold them in place and weave a thread round the stalks, taking it first over the topmost straw, then under the next, then over the one after that, and so on.

3. Finally tie the two ends of the thread together behind the star.

Alternatively, you could lay the straw crosswise on a block of wood and pin it down so you have both hands free to bind the straws together.

Cut the points of the stars to your preferred shape (Figure 60).

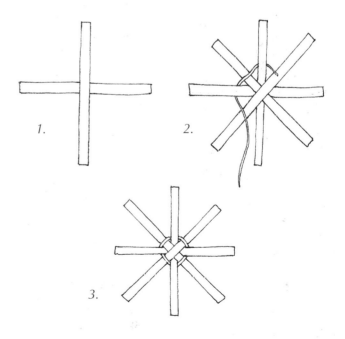

1.

2.

3.

Opposite: 50–58 Various straw stars

59 Making an 8-pointed star

16-POINTED STAR

Make two 8-pointed stars (Figures 50 and 59) and lay one on top of the other. Bind the stars together with a thread in the same way as described on page 41. The thread of one of the eight-pointed stars can be cut away.

With practice you can make this star by laying all eight stalks on top of each other at the same time, working the thread through them all and tying it up.

Altering the length and width of the stems will vary the result. Stars with a greater number of points can be made. By alternating wide and narrow, short and long, flat and hollow straw you can make innumerable varieties (Figures 50–58).

16-POINTED STAR WITH 8 LITTLE STARS

This star consists of four short and four long flat stems of straw (Figure 61). Select four wide stems and take three narrower ones for each of the eight surrounding stars (the fourth straw being already formed by the long straws of the central star).

Make an 8-pointed star with narrower straws, and tie it over the centre star.

With skill this combined star can be extended even further.

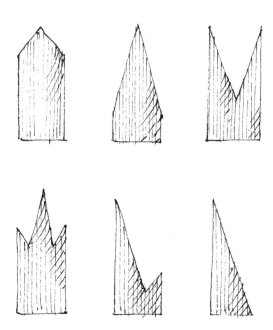

60 Star points

61 16-pointed star with 8 little stars

12-POINTED STAR

1. Cut two flat stems into three pieces each. First lay three pieces on top of each other (Figure 62).

2. Then add the other three pieces as shown in the diagram.

3. Make sure the first straw (at the bottom) is vertical, and the last straw is horizontal so that the first and last straw make a cross enclosing the other straws.

The thread with which the star is woven together comes from behind and goes over the last laid straw, under the next straw and so on.

STARS WITH 24 AND 32 POINTS

For the star with 24 points lay one 12-pointed star on another (Figure 62), weave a thread through them and tie them together. Cut off the surplus thread.

Figure 56 shows a large and a small star combined to make a star with 24 points.

VARIATION WITH 24 POINTS

The star in Figure 58 uses three wide and nine long narrow straws. Follow the steps in Figure 63.

1. Lay the three wide straws on top of each other.

2. Lay the three narrow straws behind them.

3. Lay two straws on top in the gaps between the narrow and the wide straws.

Finally bind them together.

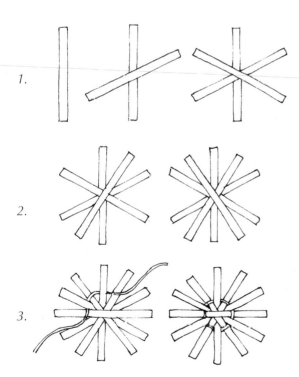

62 Making a 12-pointed star

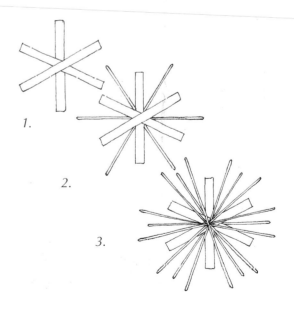

63 Variation on a 24-pointed star

43

VARIATION WITH 32 POINTS

This star is made in the same way as the one above, except that two stars with sixteen points are used. A similar star can be made from four 8-pointed stars. (Figures 57, 64–66)

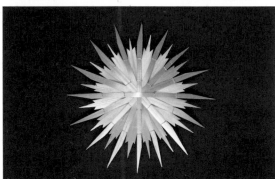

64–66 32-pointed stars

GREAT STAR WITH 64 POINTS

Figure 67 is made with 32 whole (unironed) stems of straw. In this case the straw is worked while still wet, as it is more pliable and breaks less easily.

Make a star from eight stalks by laying them crosswise on top of each other and tying them up. Make a second star in the same way.

Lay one star on top of the other, so that the rays interlock. Tie the star together with a new thread. The result is a star with 32 points.

Make a second star with 32 points, lay one star on top of the other and tie them together with new thread, to make a star with 64 points.

The straw must still be wet when you finish the ends.

67 Great star

STRAW-STAR MOBILE

The mobile in Figure 68 has a large star of David with twelve 12-pointed stars. This mobile can be hung during the time between Christmas and Epiphany (January 6). Begin with the large star of David and each day add a 12-pointed star.

For the star of David take six wet whole straws.

1. Lay three straws on top of each other to make an equilateral triangle and tie the ends together (Figure 69). With the other three straws make another triangle.

2. Lay one triangle on top of the other to make the 6-pointed star of David. Tie the stars together where they cross and suspend the mobile from four points (Figure 68).

Make the 12-pointed stars from whole straws ironed flat: since these are heavier they hang well.

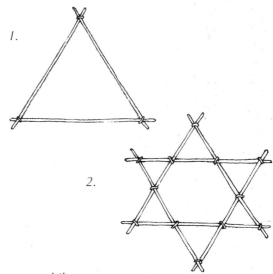

68 Straw-star mobile

69 Making a star of David

45

Paper window stars

MATERIALS
Kite paper (transparency paper) or tissue paper
Transparent glue or a glue stick
Double-sided adhesive tape
Sharp knife

Transparent window stars are made by folding each piece of paper into a single star-point and then assembling these star-points into a star.

Kite paper (transparency paper) is sufficiently transparent and is more robust than tissue paper, so it is more easily worked.

Tissue paper is less colour fast than kite paper and since transparent stars are usually left to hang for a long time, tissue-paper stars can quickly lose their colour in the increasing strength of the sunlight.

When choosing the colours remember that the patterns emerge from layering different colours of paper. For complicated stars dark colours are not suitable; use yellow, orange, pale green or pink.

Do not make the stars too small because it is more difficult to make the folds exact. The examples in this book have a diameter of 20 cm (8 in).

The proportion of the sheets is important — if altered, the pattern changes too. For example Figure 82 uses 10 × 7.5 cm (4 × 3 in) sheets while Figure 83 uses 10 × 4.5 cm (4 × 1¾ in) sheets.

Before making the star-points experiment with:

Rectangular sheets (for instance 10 × 7.5 cm, 4 × 3 in). Here the length of the sheet determines the dimensions of the star. In our examples (page 51) the star will be twice the length, that is 20 cm (8 in).

Square sheets where the diagonal determines the dimensions of the star. A sheet 7.5 × 7.5 cm (3 × 3 in) has a diagonal of a little over 10 cm (4 in) — about one third longer than the sides.

7.5 cm (3 in)

70 Square sheet

Work out beforehand how many pieces can be obtained from one large sheet to avoid waste. You can get 100 rectangular sheets (10 × 7.5 cm, 4 × 3 in) or 130 square sheets (7.5 × 7.5 cm, 3 × 3 in) out of a 75 × 102 cm (30 × 40 in) sheet of kite paper.

Make sure that the pieces are exactly the same size; to achieve this, first fold the large sheet exactly in half (with a sharp crease) and slit in two with a sharp knife. Then fold these sheets in two and cut them. Continue in this way until you have obtained the desired size. A guillotine or trimmer is very useful for this. In order to obtain a different shape of sheet, narrower, wider or longer, first cut a strip off the large sheet, so that exact measurements are obtained.

It is important to fold the sheets as exactly as possible because any divergence shows up in the final result.

The creases must be really sharp. When the same points have to be folded twice as in Figure 84 then don't make the first fold come exactly to the centre line but leave a tiny gap. Ensure that the sides come exactly together with the second fold.

Stick down all the folded parts using transparent glue or a glue stick. Non-transparent glue becomes visible when the star is hung up. Make sure that you don't use too much glue on the paper.

Finally stick the stars to the window with strips of double-sided adhesive tape. Use only very small strips and stick them to the parts where the star is least transparent (the points) then the tape will not be seen. Large pieces of tape will make the star difficult to remove without damage.

STARS FROM SQUARE PIECES

With stars made from square pieces the diagonal is the central fold.

SIMPLE 8-POINTED STAR
8 pieces of kite paper (7.5 × 7.5 cm, 3 × 3 in)

1. Fold the sheets across the diagonal so that points B and C meet. Unfold again (Figure 71).

2. Fold points *B* and *C* in to the diagonal; stick them down with a spot of glue.

3. When all eight sheets are folded in this way stick the star carefully together, with the unfolded base of the first star-point to the diagonal of the next, continuing until all the points have been stuck together (Figure 75).

10-POINTED STAR
10 pieces of kite paper (7.5 × 7.5 cm, 3 × 3 in)

Fold the star-points in the same way as before (Figure 71, steps 1 and 2).

Stick the unfolded base of the second star-point a little bit over the diagonal of the first as in Figure 72, step 2. This forms a pattern of rays in the heart of the star (Figure 76).

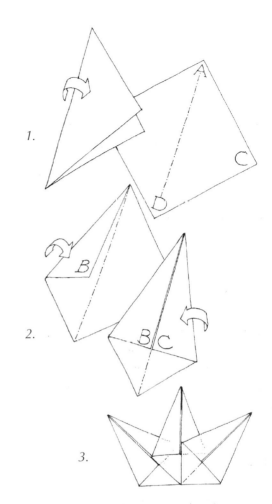

71 Making a simple star

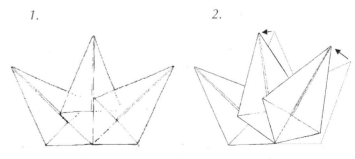

72 Making a 10-pointed star

47

8-POINTED STAR
8 pieces of kite paper (7.5 × 7.5 cm, 3 × 3 in)

This 8-pointed star is a slight variation (Figure 73).

1. Crease the diagonal, fold points *B* and *C* to the diagonal.
2. Unfold again.
3. Fold points *B* and *C* to the newly made crease, close the flaps again, and stick down securely.

Then stick the star together as in Figure 71, step 3 to result in Figure 77.

5-POINTED STAR
5 pieces of kite paper (7.5 × 7.5 cm, 3 × 3 in)

By taking five instead of eight star-points you can modify the star in Figure 77 to make Figures 78 and 79.

The overlap of each individual point of the star is no longer a half point as before, but only about 10–12 mm, 1/2 in (Figure 74). In this way a five-point motif appears in the middle (Figure 78).

10-POINTED STAR
10 pieces of kite paper (7.5 × 7.5 cm, 3 × 3 in)

With ten star-points make two 5-pointed stars and stick one on top of the other. This gives you the star in Figure 79.

Alternatively first assemble one 5-pointed star and then stick the remaining five points one by one between the points of the star.

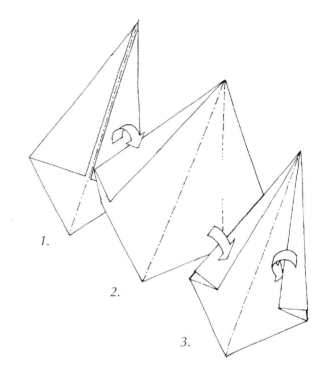

73 Making an 8-pointed star

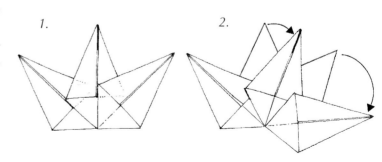

74 Making a 5-pointed star

75 Simple 8-pointed star

76 10-pointed star

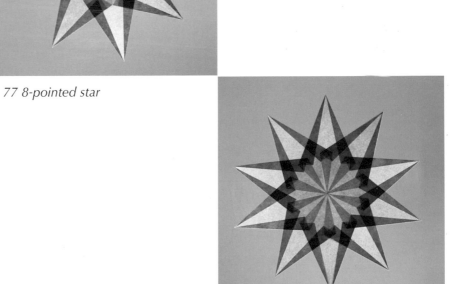

77 8-pointed star

78 5-pointed star

79 10-pointed star

49

80 11-pointed star

11-POINTED STAR
11 pieces of kite paper (7.5 × 7.5 cm, 3 × 3 in)

Fold the sheets as in Figure 73, steps 1 and 2.

1. Then fold the lower half (the part that will become the centre of the star) towards the diagonal line (Figure 81).

2. Stick the folds down.

Stick the 11 star-points together to produce the star of Figure 80.

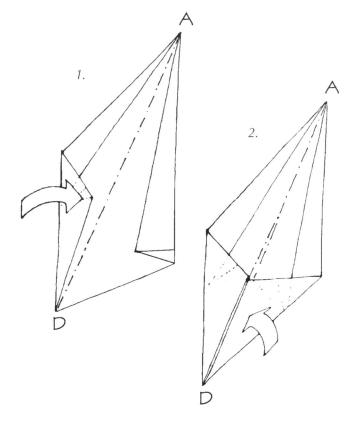

81 Making an 11-pointed star

STARS FROM RECTANGULAR PIECES

With rectangular sheets, the length of the sheet determines the dimensions of the star. Thus the diameter of the star will be 20 cm (8 in) using sheets of 10 × 7.5 cm (4 × 3 in).

TWO SIMPLE 8-POINTED STARS

STAR 1

8 pieces of kite paper (10 × 7.5 cm, 4 × 3 in)

1. Fold the sheets lengthwise and unfold them again (Figure 84).
    2. Fold the four corners in to the centre line so that a point is made above and below. Stick down the corners with glue.
    3. From the top point fold the two sides once again to the centre line. This sharp point makes one of the points of the star, while the wider lower point will be in the centre of the star.
    4. When all eight sheets have been folded in this way stick the star carefully together, with the unfolded base of the first star-point to the diagonal of the next, continuing until all the points have been stuck together (Figure 82).

STAR 2

8 pieces of kite paper (10 × 4.5 cm, 4 × 1³/4 in)

Fold in the same way as above, but with the narrower sheet, you will get the star in Figure 83.

82 Simple 8-pointed star (Star 1)

83 Simple 8-pointed star (Star 2)

Continued overleaf

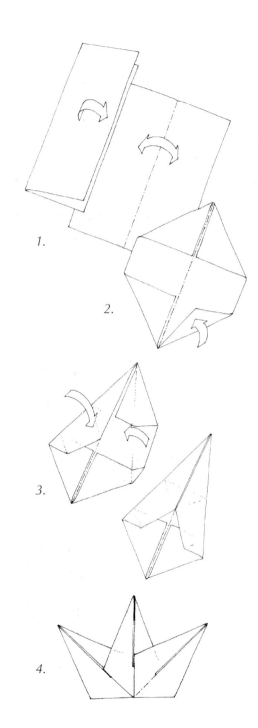

1.

2.

3.

4.

84 Making a simple 8-pointed star

STAR 1
8 pieces of kite paper (10 × 7.5 cm, 4 × 3 in)

1. Fold the sheets lengthwise and unfold them again (Figure 86).

2. Fold the two top corners in to the centre line. Unfold them again.

3. Halve the corner folds and tuck the edge inside as you fold it again.

4. Assemble the star by first using four star-points to make a 4-pointed star. Then insert the remaining points between the gaps.

Above: 85 8-pointed star (star 1)
Below: 89 8-pointed star (star 2)

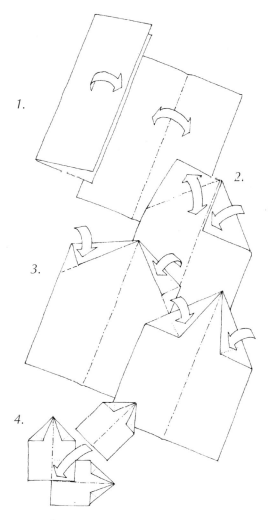

1.

2.

3.

4.

86 Making star 1

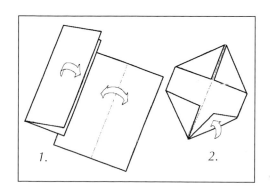

1.

2.

87

8 pieces of kite paper (10 × 7.5 cm, 4 × 3 in)

Fold each corner towards the centre line (Figure 87). Now follow Figure 88.

1. Unfold the lower corners again.

2. Fold the lower two points to the new crease and then fold inwards.

3. Fold the top flap onto the centre crease.

4. Finish by folding the other flap.

Stick together to make the star in Figure 89.

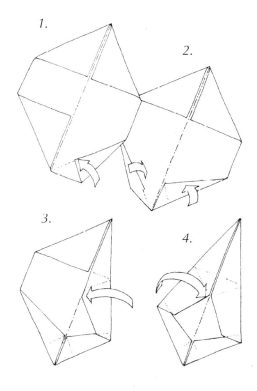

1.

2.

3.

4.

88 Making star 2

NARROW 8-POINTED STAR
8 pieces of kite paper (12 × 4.5 cm, 4³/4 × 1³/4 in)

This star looks quite different because the sheets are narrower. Don't use sheets smaller than the above measurements as they will be too difficult to work.

Follow the basic folds in Figure 92. Then follow the steps in Figure 95.
1. Fold the outside folds again.
2. Then fold them again to make a sharp point.
Stick together to make the star in Figure 96.

96 Narrow 8-pointed star

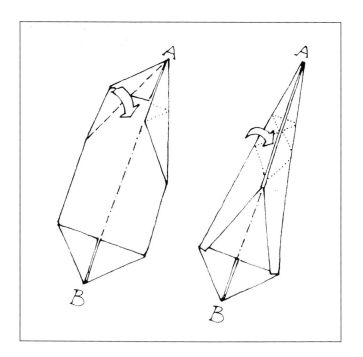

95 Making a narrow 8-pointed star

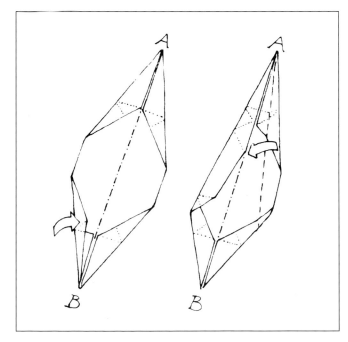

98 Making star 2

56

97 Narrow 16-pointed star (Star 1)

99 Narrow 16-pointed star (Star 2)

NARROW 16-POINTED STARS

STAR 1

6 pieces of kite paper (15 × 4.5 cm, 6 × 1³/4 in)

Fold the star-points in the same way as for the Narrow 8-pointed star.

Stick the star together as described for the previous 16-pointed star (Figures 93 and 94).

The final result can be seen in Figure 97.

STAR 2

16 pieces of kite paper (15 × 4.5 cm, 6 × 1 ³/4 in)

In this star an extra fold is added and so a larger size of paper is used (Figure 98).

1. Fold each of the corners twice.

2. Then fold the two outside corners in again to make a sharp point.

Stick together like the previous version (Figures 93 and 94) to make the star in Figure 99.

Pentagonal window stars

MATERIALS
Gold or coloured card
Tracing paper
Tissue paper
Transparent glue or a glue stick
Thread
Sharp knife or scissors
Ruler and pencil

100 Pentagonal transparency

Transparencies showing a 5-pointed star are simple for children to make and quickly give a good result. These transparencies can be hung in front of the window.

Cut out a pentagon from gold or coloured card. Different sizes of pentagon are shown on page 30 as a pattern. Draw a second pentagon inside the first at a distance of 2 cm (3/4 in) from the edge. Cut the central pentagon out of card so that a pentagonal frame is left. Do not make the frame any narrower in case the card starts to bend when the tissue paper is stuck on.

First cover the back of your frame with white tracing paper. Place a triangle of tissue paper over three corners of the pentagon joining two opposite points and completely covering the point between (Figure 101a). Stick the edges of the tissue paper along the two sides of the pentagon. Take another triangle and join the next two corners together (Figure 101b). Continue in this way until all the corners are joined up (Figure 101c). It is important that the long edge of each triangle is cut cleanly and straight, as this edge will be visible.

It is advisable to stick the tissue paper together with a tiny bit of glue or a glue stick. Inside the frame you will now have a 5-pointed star with another pentagon in the middle with the apex pointing downwards.

Finally stick a thread to the top of the frame to suspend the transparency. Be careful of sticking the transparency on to a window with double-sided adhesive tape as it may tear when you want to take it down again.

PENTAGON 1

Make a transparency as described above. When the star inside the frame is finished repeat the procedure, reducing the size of the triangles of tissue paper by 5 mm (1/4 in). In this way a second five-pointed star appears. Repeat until you reach the edge of the frame. Remember from time to time to stick the pieces of tissue paper together in the middle with a tiny bit of glue. Finish off the outside of the frame by cutting away all superfluous bits of paper.

The version described above can also be made with various colours. Just make sure the colours aren't too dark as the light will not be able to shine through.

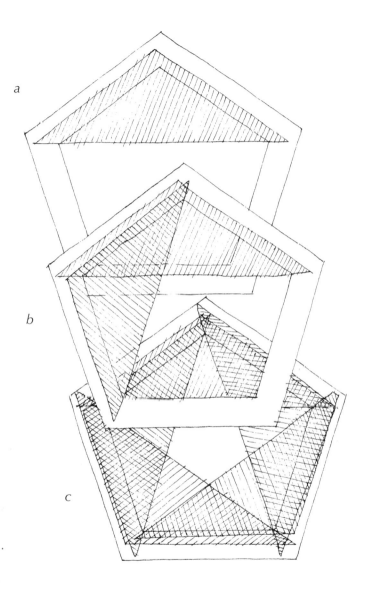

a

b

c

101 Making a pentagonal transparency

102 Pentagon 1

Pentagon 2

The frame can also be varied, as shown in Figure 103, where the surrounding frame is round. The transparent star inside the frame appears to be complicated but can be made in a very simple manner. First make a 5-pointed star as shown in Figure 100. Then take strips of tissue paper about 1 cm (3/8 in) wide and use them to join the two opposite corners of the pentagon in such a way that half of the strip is stuck over the star while the other half falls inside. Where the strip has been stuck over the existing star, a darker band will appear. Here, too, innumerable variations can be achieved. Make sure you do not use too much glue, or it may cause colour differences in the tissue paper.

103 Pentagon 2

Nativity scenes

CLAY STABLE

A clay stable can be made as simply as you wish (Figure 104). Children can make this stable by themselves.

With these simple stables the surrounding landscape creates an atmosphere. Use dark brown or green cloth and lay some stones, moss or pine cones on it. Make trees by sticking a sprig of green in a lump of clay.

You could let the children make something for each Sunday during Advent:

On the first Sunday make the stable.

On the second Sunday make some bushes and trees to go round it.

On the third Sunday make some sheep.

And on the fourth Sunday the people: Joseph, Mary and the shepherds, and for Christmas, the angel and the child.

Make the figures in one piece. Do not make arms, legs and head and then stick them on to the body because once the clay dries the separate parts are likely to fall off.

Once the stable is dry it can be painted if desired.

104 Clay stable

Nativity Scene

Materials

White and brown unspun sheep's wool
Pink cotton knit
Coloured scraps of cloth and felt
Scraps of fur
Unspun wool or camel hair

Nativity figures

1. For each figure work a tuft of teased white wool into a firm roll approximately 9 cm (3 1/2 in) long.

2. Form a round head at one end.

3. Wrap a piece of cotton knit round it and tie it off to make the head.

4. Make a fairly close-fitting garment from a thicker woollen material or felt to cover the rest of the roll of wool, so that the figure can stand.

5. Gather the cloth in at the neck.

Mary has a robe of red felt, with a cloak made of a square piece of blue cloth or felt.

6. Drape the cloak round her head and fasten with a few stitches at the head and the neck (Figure 105).

7. The hands are made of some teased sheep's wool covered with cotton knit. Sew them to the inside of the cloak.

Draw in the eyes and mouth with a fine pencil.

Joseph and the shepherds have capes of cloth or fur. Secure these at the neck and at the centre front with a few stitches. A stick can then be inserted between the cape and the body (Figure 105, step 7).

The hair is made of teased brown sheep's wool secured with the hat.

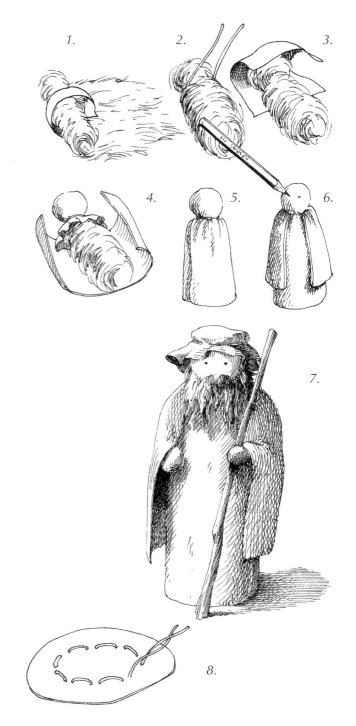

105 Making nativity figures

8. The hat is made from a round piece of felt. You can shape the hat by gathering it, then sew it on to the head with a few stitches.

The *child* is made in the same way as the other dolls, only a little smaller. When the head is finished wrap the rest of the body in a cloth of light-coloured material, flannel or felt. Secure the cloth with a few stitches.

Make a simple *sheep* from a rectangular piece of fur or fleece. Roll this in from the narrow end. Sew up at the bottom and if necessary at the ends using a leatherwork needle. Tie off about one third to make the head. Now clip the sheep to give it a good shape. Make ears of soft leather or felt and sew them on.

Ox and ass (Figure 106). Turn in the ends of a little skein of carded unspun wool. From this shape a lying ass with a few loose stitches and a fine thread. Make the ears by gently pulling out the wool. For the ox, camel hair or light brown, teased sheep's wool is ideal.

The *stable* can be built of pieces of bark and twigs nailed or stuck together. Use single large pieces of bark for the roof. The stable can then be furnished with straw, moss, plants, stones and so on.

106 Ox and ass

63

PIPE-CLEANER SHEEP

MATERIALS
4 pipe-cleaners
White unspun wool
Darning needle
Crochet hook No. 3 (US C/2 or D/3)
Old scissors or pliers
Glue

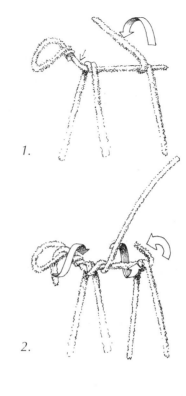

1. For the head of the sheep bend the end of a pipe-cleaner round two fingers and twist it round the neck (Figure 107). Make a kink for the neck.

For the forelegs bend a pipe-cleaner round the body; and do the same for the hind legs. Cut the feet to shape only when the sheep is completely finished.

2. Use the fourth pipe-cleaner to give the frame more stability and to lengthen the tail. Bend the end of the first pipe-cleaner to the front and twist it round the body.

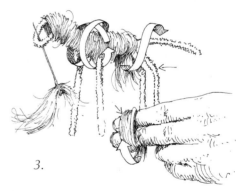

3. Tease a bit of wool out and begin working it round the sheep at the stomach. After each turn let go of the tuft to avoid getting it twisted. Continue working round the sheep evenly from the body to the head and back again to the hind parts until it is thick enough.

Keep winding the wool to the last fibre; this will prevent it from unravelling. Do not work to the very end of the nose, or the wool will slip off.

Work the shoulders and the hind legs as follows: hold one end of the piece of wool tightly on to the left shoulder, take the wool down behind the left fore leg and back up obliquely over the chest, over the neck, crosswise over the breast to the right foreleg, back behind it and so on. In this way you form a figure of eight. Do not work the wool too tightly and make sure that it

107 Making a pipe-cleaner sheep

lies flat on the back. Work the hindquarters in the same way. Do not make the head too thick.

The *nose:* Thread a bit of wool through the darning needle and secure the nose. Cover the front part also with wool.

The *tail:* Push the wool towards the hindquarters so that the tail pipe-cleaner stands free. Wind a tuft of wool over half of the pipe cleaner. Bend the pipe-cleaner back halfway, so that the end of the tail is covered with wool. The tail should now be 2.5 cm (1 in) long. Finish off the bent-back tail with another tuft of wool, giving the tail a nice shape.

The *legs:* Push the wool of the body up a bit and wind good thin tufts of wool round the legs about halfway down. Put some glue on the lower half of the legs and continue to wind on wool. Allow the glue to dry properly and finish off by cutting the legs to the right size.

4. The *ears:* Wind a bit of wool evenly round two fingers and remove. Thrust the crochet hook carefully through the head where shown in Figure 107. Catch the wool in the hook and, pressing your fingers on the other side of the head, pull the hook through.

Take both ears between your thumb and forefinger and rub them into shape. Let the ears hang and fasten them with needle and thread.

You can make an *ox* and *ass* in the same way, following the pipe-cleaner shape shown in Figure 106.

108 A pipe-cleaner sheep

Geometric decorations

THREE-DIMENSIONAL FOIL SHAPES

MATERIALS
Gold foil
Sharp scissors or a sharp knife
Sharp pencil
Glue
Ruler

TETRAHEDRON AND CUBE

A tetrahedron is a regular solid figure contained by four regular (equilateral) triangles (Figure 109). Enlarge the pattern of Figure 110 to double its size. It is easiest to photocopy the pattern or construct it on a loose sheet of paper. This avoids unnecessary lines and marks appearing on the foil.

Lay the sheet of paper with the copied pattern on the back of the gold foil, and stick it on with two bits of adhesive tape so that it will not slip. Then draw the whole shape on to the foil.

Remove the paper and cut the shape out of the foil. To get good sharp creases fold and unfold the crease a few times before sticking down.

Spread the glue thinly on both surfaces to be stuck. Wait until the glue is nearly dry and then stick the tetrahedron together, sticking a suspension thread to the inside before closing it. Tie a few knots at the bottom of the thread so that it will not slip out of the tetrahedron. Make sure that the corners join together as exactly as possible because the glued parts are not easy to unstick.

109 Tetrahedron and cube

A cube consists of six squares. The pattern in Figure 111 is half size. Stick the cube together in the same way as the tetrahedron.

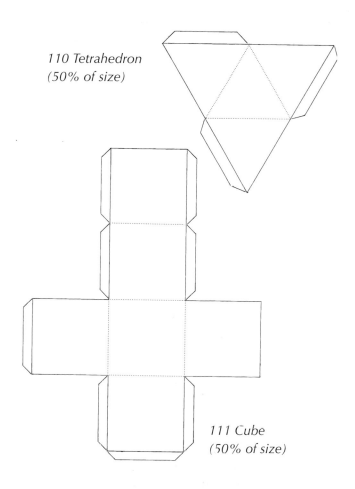

110 Tetrahedron
(50% of size)

111 Cube
(50% of size)

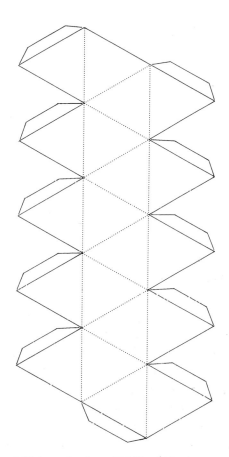

113 Icosahedron (60% of size)

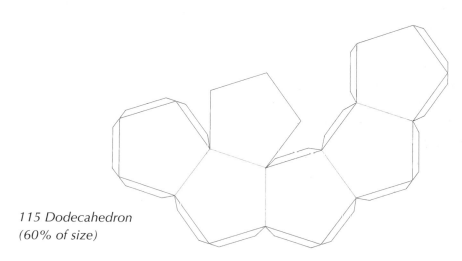

115 Dodecahedron
(60% of size)

112 Icosahedron

114 Dodecahedron

ICOSAHEDRON

The icosahedron consists of twenty equilateral triangles (Figure 112). In Figure 113 the pattern is shown unfolded at 60% of true size.

The construction of the icosahedron is as for the tetrahedron (p. 66).

Fold all the lines before beginning to glue the model, as this is no longer possible afterwards.

Leave one of the triangles open to the end, so that you can even out any irregularities from the inside using a pencil.

DODECAHEDRON

This shape consists of twelve regular pentagons (Figure 114). Figure 115 shows a pattern at 60% of true size for six pentagons, which make up half of the dodecahedron.

When the six pentagons are stuck together they make a bowl. Two such bowls fit exactly together (Figure 39, page 32), but in this model only the lower bowl needs flaps, not both bowls.

Stick the bottom half together completely, and when sticking the top half together, leave the 'lid' open.

If necessary the sticking edges can be pressed with a pencil from the inside and any irregularities removed. Before folding down the lid stick a thread to the inside of one of the corners.

116 Star

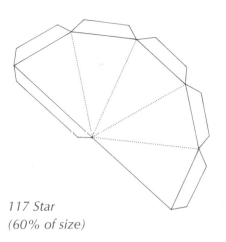

117 Star
(60% of size)

STAR

A three-dimensional star can be made using a dodecahedron as a base (Figure 116).

Make twelve pentagonal pyramids, the base of each being the same size as that of the dodecahedron (Figure 117), and stick one pyramid on to each pentagon of the dodecahedron.

In the same way a three-dimensional star can be made from an icosahedron, in this case use twenty three-sided pyramids.

THREE-DIMENSIONAL STRAW SHAPES

MATERIALS
Straw
Metal ruler
Sharp knife
Adhesive tape
Glue
Strong paper
Scissors
Thread

DODECAHEDRONS

This dodecahedron consists of twelve regular 5-pointed stars (Figure 118). As a guide to determining the size of this decoration: the *side* of a pentagon is 3 cm (1¼ in); the *diagonal* of a 5-pointed star is 5 cm (2 in); the *diameter* of the whole dodecahedron will be about 8 cm (3¼ in).

Use flat ironed straw (see Straw stars on page 41). Cut the straw into thin strips with the help of a sharp knife and a metal ruler.

For a dodecahedron sixty (12 × 5) strips are needed. So calculate how many strips you can get out of one straw to avoid waste.

For this three-dimensional form it is very important that the 5-pointed stars are exactly the same size. A handy way of making the strips all the same size is to mark off the desired length on some drawing paper. Lay all the strips on the paper between the marks. Stick the straws together with some adhesive tape. Clip them to size with a pair of scissors along the marks.

118 Straw dodecahedrons

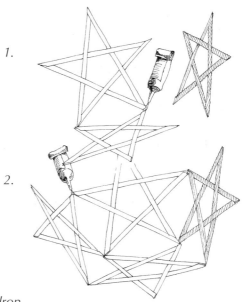

119 Making a straw dodecahedron

Construct a 5-pointed star of the desired size on a piece of paper, using Figure 37, page 30. Use this as a template for sticking the star together.

Take five strips and lay them with the shiny side down. Do this for each 5-pointed star.

Following the diagram in Figure 119, apply a little glue to the ends of two strips, one on the shiny side, one on the dull side (use a tube with a very fine nozzle, for example model-building glue). Allow the glue to dry a bit and then stick the end of the other straw on to it firmly. When interwoven as shown the five strips make a 5-pointed star. To add the third straw, apply glue to one of the ends of the two straws that are stuck together, allow it to dry a bit and stick on the third straw. In the same way stick on the last two strips.

Quickly check that the star is regular by laying it on the pattern (Figure 37). If necessary adjust the points before the glue sets. Make all the stars in this way and allow them to set.

Now join the stars together to form a dodecahedron by applying a little glue to all five points of the first three stars. Allow the glue to dry a bit.

1. Stick two stars together at two points (Figure 119, step 1). Place one of these stars on a block of wood as a base and ease the other star up so that the third star can be joined to the pair.

Apply glue to the points of the next three stars and allow to dry.

2. Stick these stars to the free points of the three stars already joined. Now half of the dodecahedron is finished.

Proceed in the same way until the whole star is finished. When you are sticking on the last star use a little more glue on one of the points so that you can attach a gold suspension thread.

Figure 120 shows how to make each side of the dodecahedron a pentagon with a 5-pointed star inside it. Stick all the stars together as described above, then add the links between the star-points which make up the pentagon.

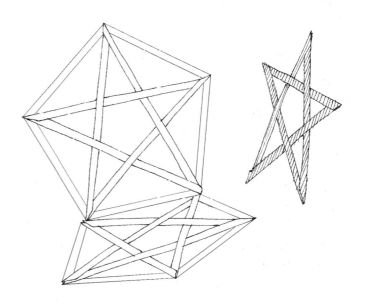

120 Making a straw dodecahedron

Figure 121 shows a smaller dodecahedron inside a larger one. For this, two complete dodecahedrons are needed, the smaller being less than two thirds of the larger.

Paint the smaller dodecahedron with a little red varnish to make it more visible or use darker straw for the smaller star.

Place the smaller dodecahedron inside the larger one before the last two stars are stuck together. Add a thread joining the smaller dodecahedron to the larger one, ensuring that the distance between them is correct.

STRAW BALL

Iron the straw flat (see page 141) and cut it into strips about 3 mm (1/8 in) wide. The ball in Figure 122 consists of eight rings.

1. Because the rings are all stuck over each other the diameter of the innermost ring must be a fraction smaller than that of the next one and so on. As the difference is scarcely perceptible the best way is to stick the two ends of the innermost ring with slightly more overlap than those of the next (Figure 123).

2. Make the first two rings, allow them to dry fully and then stick them together in the form of a cross, making sure that the joints of the ring don't coincide exactly. The glue of these rings stuck together must now dry fully because this is the foundation for the rest.

3. Make the remaining six rings and allow them to dry too. Then fill up the gaps between the cross in the following way: begin by sticking two rings in the middle between the cross.

4. Once this is dry stick the remaining four rings in the intervening spaces.

121 Small dodecahedron inside larger dodecahedron

122 Straw ball

Allow the glue to dry properly, then glue a piece of thread on to one of the rings. The positioning of the thread produces different effects: if it placed as in Figure 122 it produces the greatest effect of depth; if attached to the cross-points of the rings the ball has vertical stripes; when attached halfway between cross-points the ball has horizontal stripes. Several identical balls can create the impression that they are all different.

An extra ring placed at right angles round the other rings can be the beginning of a whole series of variations. The breadth of the rings can also be varied; indeed you can place rings touching each other all the way round so that a true ball is formed.

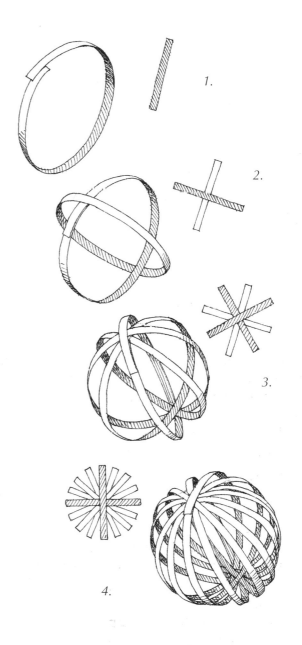

123 Making a straw ball

Further reading

Adolphi, Sybille, *Making Fairy Tale Scenes,* Floris Books, Edinburgh.

—, *Making Flower Children,* Floris Books, Edinburgh

—, *Making More Flower Children,* Floris Books, Edinburgh.

Aeppli, Willi, *Care and Development of the Human Senses,* Steiner Press, London.

Anschütz, Marieke, *Children and their Temperaments,* Floris Books, Edinburgh.

Barz, Brigitte, *Festivals with Children,* Floris Books, Edinburgh.

Berger, Petra, *Feltcraft,* Floris Books, Edinburgh.

Berger, Thomas, *The Christmas Craft Book,* Floris Books, Edinburgh.

Berger, Thomas & Petra, *Crafts through the Year,* Floris Books, Edinburgh.

—, *The Gnome Craft Book,* Floris Books, Edinburgh.

Clouder, Chris & Martyn Rawson, *Waldorf Education,* Floris Books, Edinburgh.

Crossley, Diana, *Muddles, Puddles and Sunshine,* Hawthorn Press, Stroud.

Dancy, Rahima Baldwin, *You are your Child's First Teacher,* Celestial Arts.

Evans, Russell, *Helping Children to Overcome Fear,* Hawthorn Press, Stroud.

Grunelius, Elisabeth, *Early Childhood Education and the Waldorf School Plan,* Waldorf Monographs, New York.

Guéret, Frédérique, *Magical Window Stars,* Floris Books, Edinburgh.

Harwood, A.C. *The Way of a Child,* Steiner Press, London.

Jaffke, Freya, *Work and Play in Early Childhood,* Floris Books, Edinburgh & Anthroposophic Press, New York.

Jenkinson, Sally, *The Genius of Play,* Hawthorn Press, Stroud.

König, Karl, *The First Three Years of the Child,* Floris Books, Edinburgh.

Kornberger, Horst, *The Power of Stories,* Floris Books, Edinburgh.

Kutsch, Irmgard and Brigitte Walden, *Autumn Nature Activities for Children,* Floris Books, Edinburgh.

—, *Spring Nature Activities for Children,* Floris Books, Edinburgh.

—, *Summer Nature Activities for Children,* Floris Books, Edinburgh.

—, *Winter Nature Activities for Chidren,* Floris Books, Edinburgh.

Kraul, Walter, *Earth, Water, Fire and Air,* Floris Books, Edinburgh.

Leeuwen, M van & J Moeskops, *The Nature Corner,* Floris Books, Edinburgh.

Mellon, Nancy, *Storytelling with Children,* Hawthorn Press, Stroud.

Meyer, Rudolf, *The Wisdom of Fairy Tales,* Floris Books, Edinburgh.

Müller, Brunhild, *Painting with Children,* Floris Books, Edinburgh.

Neuschütz, Karin, *Sewing Dolls,* Floris Books, Edinburgh.

Oldfield, Lynne, *Free to Learn,* Hawthorn Press, Stroud.

Petrash, Carol, *Earthwise: Environmental Crafts and Activities with Young Children,* Floris Books, Edinburgh & Gryphon House, Maryland.

Rawson, Martyn & Michael Rose, *Ready to Learn,* Hawthorn Press, Stroud.

Reinckens, Sunnhild, *Making Dolls,* Floris Books, Edinburgh.

Santer, Ivor, *Green Fingers and Muddy Boots,* Floris Books, Edinburgh.

Schmidt, Dagmar & Freya Jaffke, *Magic Wool,* Floris Books, Edinburgh.

Sealey, Maricristin, *Kinder Dolls,* Hawthorn Press, Stroud.

Steiner, Rudolf, *The Education of the Child in the Light of Anthroposophy,* Steiner Press, London, & Anthroposophic Press, New York.

Taylor, Michael, *Finger Strings,* Floris Books, Edinburgh.

Thomas, Anne & Peter, *The Children's Party Book,* Floris Books, Edinburgh

Wolck-Gerche, Angelika, *Creative Felt,* Floris Books, Edinburgh.

—, *More Magic Wool,* Floris Books, Edinburgh.

—, *Papercraft,* Floris Books, Edinburgh.

Christmas and winter themed story and picture books (all from Floris Books)

Beskow, Elsa, *Ollie's Ski Trip*

—, *Peter and Lotta's Christmas*

Drescher, Daniela, *Little Fairy's Christmas*

Klaassen, Sandra, *Uan the Little Lamb*

Koopmans, Loek, *The Little Christmas Tree*

Lindgren, Astrid, *A Calf for Christmas*

Muller, Gerda, *Winter* (boardbook)

von Olfers, Sibylle, *Story of the Snow Children*

Sehlin, Gunhild, *Mary's Little Donkey*

Tyler, Brenda, *The Tomtes of Hilltop Wood*

Verschuren, Ineke, *The Christmas Story Book*

Wenz-Viëtor, Else, *The Christmas Angels*

—, *On Christmas Eve*

Resources

SOURCES FOR MAGIC WOOL AND NATURAL MATERIALS

AUSTRALIA
Morning Star
www.morningstarcrafts.com.au

Winterwood Toys
www.winterwoodtoys.com.au

NORTH AMERICA
The Waldorf Early Childhood Association of North America maintains an online list of suppliers at:
www.waldorfearlychildhood.org/sources.asp

UK
Myriad Natural Toys
www.myriadonline.co.uk

WALDORF SCHOOLS

In 2010 there are almost 1000 Waldorf schools and 1,500 kindergartens in over 60 countries around the world. Up-to-date information can be found on any of the websites below.

AUSTRALIA
Association of Rudolf Steiner Schools in Australia, PO Box 111, Robertson, NSW 2577
rssa@bigpond.com
www.steineroz.com

NEW ZEALAND
Federation of Rudolf Steiner Schools, PO Box 888, Hastings, Hawkes Bay
waldorf@voyager.nz
www.rudolfsteinerfederation.org.nz

NORTH AMERICA
Association of Waldorf Schools of North America, 3911 Bannister Road, Fair Oaks, CA 95628
awsna@awsna.org
www.whywaldorfworks.org

SOUTH AFRICA
Southern African Federation of Waldorf Schools, PO Box 280, Plumstead 7801
federation@waldorf.org.za
www.waldorf.org.za

UK
Steiner Schools Fellowship, Kidbrooke Park, Forest Row, RH18 5JB
mail@swsf.org.uk
www.steinerwaldorf.org.uk

Thomas and Petra Berger
ISBN 978–086315–828–5

Petra Berger
ISBN 978–086315–720–2

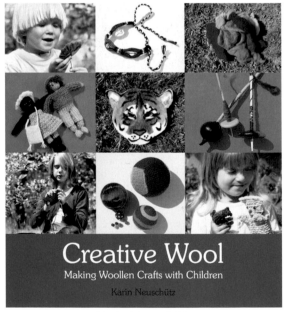

Karin Neuschütz
ISBN 978–086315–800–1

Angelika Wolk-Gerche
ISBN 978–086315–678–6

www.florisbooks.co.uk

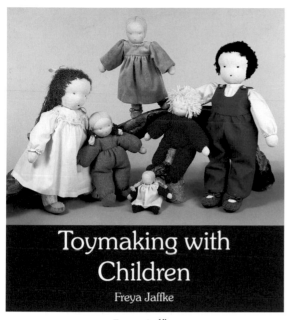

Toymaking with Children

Freya Jaffke

Freya Jaffke
ISBN 978–086315–769–1

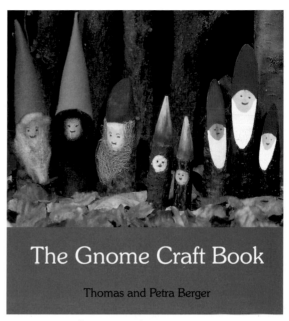

The Gnome Craft Book

Thomas and Petra Berger

Thomas and Petra Berger
ISBN 978–086315–721–9

The Nature Corner

Celebrating the year's cycle with seasonal tableaux

M. van Leeuwen and J. Moeskops

M. Van Leeuwen and J. Moeskops
ISBN 978–086315–721–9

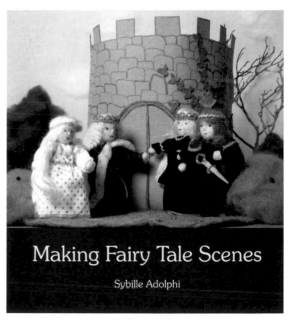

Making Fairy Tale Scenes

Sybille Adolphi

Sybille Adolphi
ISBN 978–086315–718–9

www.florisbooks.co.uk

Papercraft
Angelika Wolk-Gerche

Angelika Wolk-Gerche
ISBN 978–086315–638–0

Magical Window Stars
Frédérique Guéret

Frédérique Gueret
ISBN 978–086315–494–2

Magic Wool
Creative Pictures and Tableaux with Natural Sheep's Wool
Freya Jaffke

Freya Jaffke
ISBN 978–086315–829–2

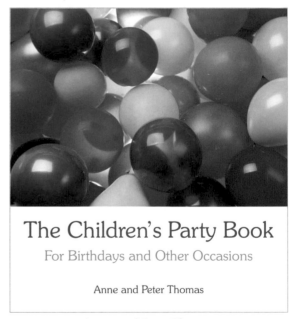

The Children's Party Book
For Birthdays and Other Occasions

Anne and Peter Thomas

Anne and Peter Thomas
ISBN 978–086315–639–7

www.florisbooks.co.uk